From the heart

Sally Whitaker

Presentation by *BookLeaf Publishing*

Web: www.bookleafpub.com

E-mail: info@bookleafpub.com

ISBN: 9789357440707

First edition 2023

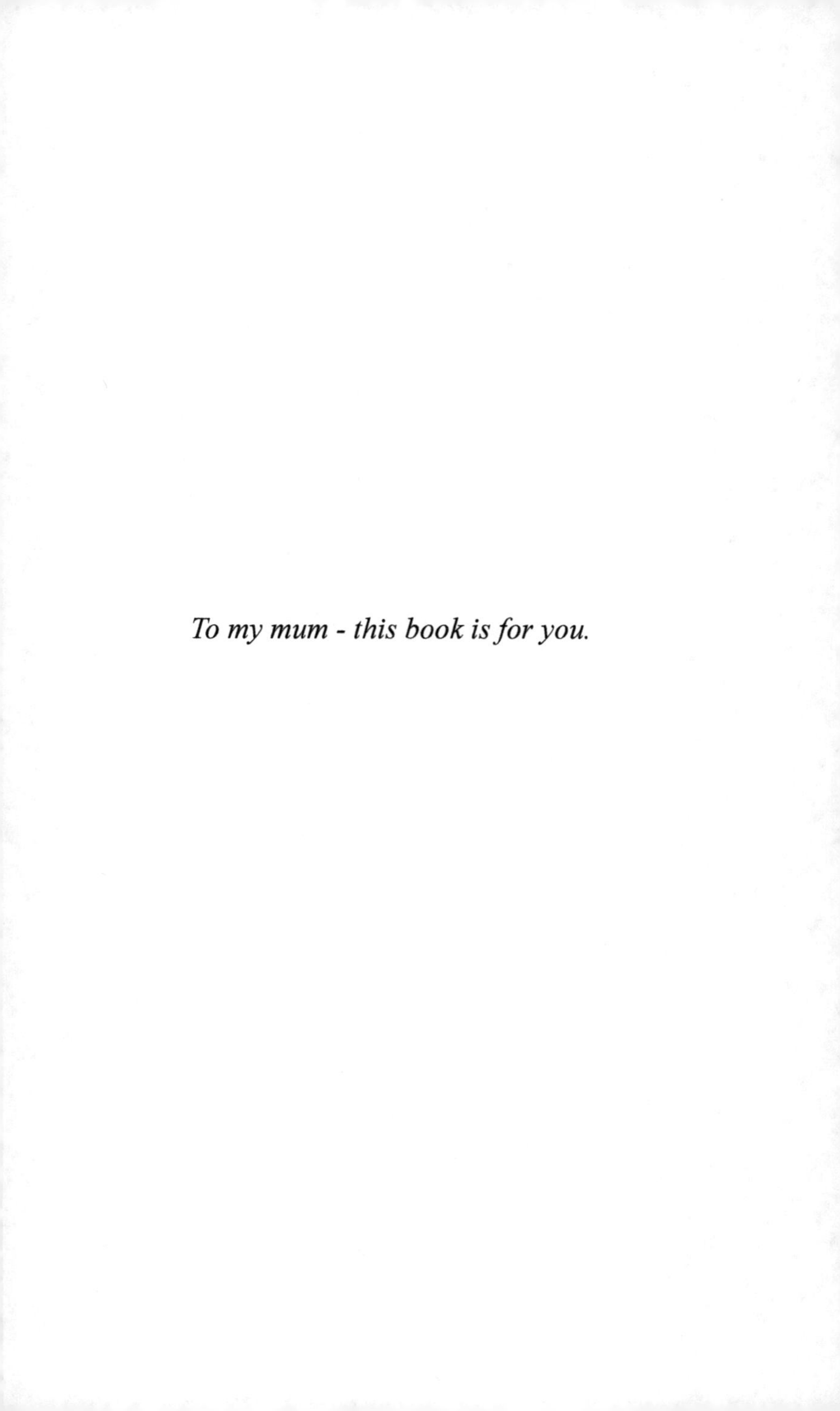

To my mum - this book is for you.

ACKNOWLEDGEMENT

Ian Whitaker.
Phoebe Grace Whitaker.
Caroline Madden.
Emma Spindley.
Jennifer Hannah.
Sandra Hannah.
Hugh Lewis.
All my other friends and family.

Thanks all for believing in me.

Waves and the heart

The waves upon the seashore crash upon the
rocks; forever leaving marks.
The permanent inscriptions leave behind history
and imprinted memories.
See the white-water rapids grow increasingly
higher, during a storm; releasing akin to
emotions being spilled; and allowed to freefall
and flow infinitely by the heart.

Two seemingly different forces of nature – the
waves and the heart, but also the same. Two
beautiful natural mechanisms that co-exist in
humanity; however, additionally commanding
the invariable liberations, of each other. The
waves and the heart everlastingly bonded in
reciprocal outlook.

Sentiments of the heart; likewise, the waves
compel liberty, acknowledgment and
furthermore recognition of necessity; in order to
accomplish innate and effortless emotive
proclamation. Restrained tolerance can precede
into anomalous phenomenon such as anguish
and gargantuan emissions of unexpended
sensations. Encouragement and admiration of all

nature's temperaments heralds affection and
collaboration inside a disenchanted human race.

My mum - The perpetual flower

The bud flourished from a new-born into an amorous and nurturing bloom.
Fragrant redolent aroma lavished the ambience with adoration and inexhaustible empathy.
Misjudged on occasion, nonetheless unbreakable plus gratifying unreservedly through its existence.

Regardless of adversities the blossom bloomed and sustained her amiable fragrance entirely. The uncompromised potency of the flower certainly eternal; considering a mother's affection is eternally furnished and flourishing straight from memoirs and sentiment.

Mothers are perpetual flowers; embrace them with complete adoration. Sometime memoirs of the elite bloom will be all that survives. Pamper the bud and nurture it forever more.

The rainbow

The rainbow materialised from nowhere. Not sufficient a shower, not excessive streams of sunlight. Billows of clouds, a little blue sky. Just a truthful and hopeful pondering from a virtuous sensitive heart. The kaleidoscopic rainbow then materialised. A deluge of sentiment developed in the soul and tumbled from the windows of the soul. Exhilaration and liberation transpired as assurance that living affairs will recuperate and become delightful when allocated patience and acknowledgement. Albeit a brief demonstration, unwavering for a solitary twenty instants; the dazzling and intense tint afforded contentment and cosiness intended for anguished individuals. Appreciated rainbow; cheers mum.

Friends forever

Friendship beholds all beating hearts.
Reality of devotion preserves contentment.
Icicles disintegrate with warmth of intimacy.
Everlasting love showers eternally.
Nothing can rival authentic affection.
Delve deep and you shall acquire.
Subtle fondness is friendship.

Forget the past. Forthwith is paramount.
Overtime florets of compelling emotions
materialise.
Remember the positives.
Expel all negatives.
Varied individuals come together.
Experiences and memories made.
Remember you are a friend forever.

Love you

Love is greatest when it is reciprocal.
Our connection eternally endures.
Visible love is akin to an eternal blossom. Never
shrinking and leaving imprints upon hearts and
minds.
Everlasting colour in the sphere formed with
your affection and devotion.

Your outright adoration reflected rearward to
you in answer.
Overflowing with empathy and eternally
offering more.
Understated amorous memories given to cherish
forever. I love you.

Seventy four

Seventy four is known as a figure of blessing
and favourable opulence. This figure was
unknowingly steadfast throughout your
Prescence on earth.

Fortune bestowed on you heirs and assigns.
Divinity knew you had immeasurable devotion
and desire to contribute unreservedly.
Seventy four years as a kin and relation,
everyone fortuitous to enjoy you and your
inexhaustible affection and charitable psyche.

Now go with peace. Eternally seventy four.

Amazing mum

Amazing elegance. Fascinating charisma.
Maternal, in every sense of word.
Awesome finesse in all executed obligations.
Zen and harmony to cease arising altercations.
Incredibly brave, and positively devoted to
relaxing any family disputes.
Nothing out lasts your amorous and
unconditional nurturing love.
Genuine and down to earth like a tree rooted
within the deep soil.

Merry and amiable to every human being.
Understated but also like a bloom which has
thus far blossomed perfectly.
Many thanks for being amazing and also for
being my mum.

I sit and ponder

I sit and ponder,
how is it in yonder?

Is heaven abound with perpetual fluorescent
glow?
Do heavenly beings promote rolling with the
flow?

I sit and ponder,
do spiritual beings as unique as you, go for a
wander?

Do clouds get fluffed by cherubs looking after
newly fledging angels?
Do you all sit around tables, telling fables?

I sit and ponder,
Do you still have dark hair, or are you now the
hair colour bronder?

The day you left

The day you left, our hearts shattered into
microscopic irreparable fragments.
Heaven gathered the finest individual they could
acquire.
Everything was hushed, before resounding
shrieks and hearty tears arose.

Don't leave us parted our lips emphatically.
Please return to us.
Absolutely, we wanted to deny, but you
appeared content and at peace.
Yes, our appreciation of you will never perish,
nor will the precious memoirs.

Your beauty, grace, dignity and utter devotion
will never fail to keep us afloat.
Outpouring of love, honour and respect has been
flowing since you left.
Understanding has ensued; peace and harmony
is completely outweighs suffering.

Licence to commemorate you we now possess;
use it we must.
Everything is now distinct; however also still the
same.

For your affection still remains, in our hearts and
our intellect.
Thank you for everything, our power, our hero.

It is not your fault

When demise punches its weight within your
life, know it is not your fault.
Sentiments of rejection, culpability, irritation
and sorrow are absolutely natural.

Never criticise oneself for admiring and losing.
It is not your fault.
Out of nowhere support and adoration gleams
through from close friends.
Thoughts can engulf oneself; nonetheless, this is
natural. Let emotions flow.

Years fly by, memories never dim and vanish.
Overall, acceptance of no guilt is what is
necessary. Demise is not your fault.
Understand the rollercoaster, the twists and
turns, and embrace them.
Rally around your relatives and those that care.
The love will multiply.

Fear not the future, seize the day and be noble
and steadfast - you are strong.
Amazing memories will flood your mind. This is
to remind you, it's not your fault.

Understand it is not your fault, embrace the love
and keep your head held high.
Love and comfort is in the environment - grasp
it and retain it.
Those departed love you eternally.

Heart break

Heightened emotions twist the heart and cause it
to shatter.
Extra sensitive layers peeling back and back.
Artistic ways of trying to hide emotion and not
crumble.
Rising tensions cause eruptions in the heart and
mind.
Tidal waves of emotion through heart break take
place.

Branches of love and hope appear and grow.
Racing thoughts and emotions calm down with
embracing attraction.
Each and every day, seek support and share.
Always seek love; and give empathy in return.
Keep sharing and caring, a heart break shared
can be a heart break solved.

Life is life

Life is for accepting challenge and strife and
being rigorous in affection.
It can be arduous and cumbersome, but can
benefit oneself too.
Feel your emotions and embrace the offerings of
nature.
Eventful activity grants alacrity and graceful
living and memories.

Inside your soul you have power, capability and
infinite ability to flourish in life.
Sound out resoundingly your inner tenacity, and
do it with satisfaction and pride.

Live, laugh, love. Life is too abbreviated to
anguish and wistful.
Individualise life and craft it how you aspire it
too.
Fairness and equality are key. Let them exude
from within.
Extenuate the positive and eliminate the
negative, find your inner peace.

My Angel

My mother is my angel.
You may know how that feels.

A celestial being, unrestrained in having desired
movements and passions.
Never deficient or desirous for anything.
Greatness is never distant in nature.
Everlasting allure and affection is emanated
forevermore.
Life with an angel is beautiful and exceptional.
Embrace it and take comfort in it.

Courage

Courage is a magnificent power to possess.
Our consciences carry the ability to value
courage and use it.
Universal strength and earth vibes are Avast and
accessible for individual use.
Reap the dividends of courage through
fearlessness and positive living.
Ability to delve deep and find the courage you
crave may seem difficult.
Give yourself time and support, you shall
acquire the fearlessness you desire.
Earths energy and opportunity provides ability to
use courage, so go for it, use it.

Proud of you

Proudness be stills my beating heart.
Rendered our minds racing with memories and
embracing love; you did.
Our hearts conclusively shattered into a million
pieces upon the death of you.
Underestimated was the power of loss; however
not how proud we are of you.
Determination was your strength, your grace and
beauty. Proud of you.

Our world collapsed when you perished, but we
are proud of you.
Fires of passion ignite upon thoughts of you and
your being.

You were bold, fearless, upstanding, honest,
cooperative, beautiful and fair.
Owned your desires, your feelings and wishes
within your life, you certainly did.
Understand, wholeheartedly, I am proud of you.

Beautiful spirit

Beautiful spirit, you have no limit.
Life and living was completely within your
remit.

Fantastic memories and emotions bubble up to
the surface.
The feelings etch themselves in psyche, much
like a furnace.

They say beauty is in the eye of the beholder;
The truth is when I think of you, I am a beauty
stockholder.

Again, beautiful spirit, you have no limit.
Thank you mum, for giving me a snippet.

Sepsis awareness

Sense the signs; fear not to approach it.
Evident confusion, high heart rate and fever.
Persist in getting it investigated if you need to; it
could save a life.
Shivering, short of breath; time to dial 999.
Infection which is active; query sepsis; save a
stitch in time.
Sepsis awareness, it's about speed and time.
Never be afraid to query sepsis and dial 999.

Queen of my heart

Queen of my heart.
United we still are, despite being a fair distance
apart.
Even when time stood still; our sentiments of
you never depreciated from within.
Evade our sight you may; our hearts and your
image will never fade away.
Never once did you fail us, you were amazing.
Queen of my heart.

Of course, when you departed, we felt broken
and shattered.
Furthermore, you still didn't lose your status.
You are the Queen of my heart.

Memories remain, and survive within, for
eternity.
Your strong sense of compassion continues to
fill the air and our lives.

Heaven gained a complete angel the day you left
the earth.
Earth lost part of its salt, part of its beauty, and
became a little more dull.

Absolutely your power of love, however, still
continues to remain.
Reality sets in; pain radiates throughout the
sorrowful souls.
Time passing aside, you are still Queen of my
heart.

Loving grandma

Loving grandma, that was what you once where.
Overarching my daughter with love, tenderness
and great care.
Vigour is what you had in life, your spark never
exited your eyes.
Imagining my daughter now growing up without
you, is hard to bare.
Never did I imagine my princess would only
have you until she was just five.
Giving everything you had, was all you ever did.
You powerful grandma, you.

Granting and exuding affection for Phoebe was
your aim. Your love shone bright.
Radiating from your soul, was heavenly beauty
and perpetual light.
Angels gathered and made sure you drifted away
peacefully.
Never did I know, nor want to, how drastic a life
change it would be without you.
Devoting your whole life to family was what
you desired, and it clearly showed.
My heart continues to sing, and remains proud
of you and your life.

Always and forever will I thank you, for being
my daughters grandma.

In the end

In the end, you maintained grace, bravery and
dignity.
Nothing stopped you from being yourself. You
just kept on going.

The world was lucky to share seventy four years
with you.
Heaven clearly needed a special lady like you.
Everything has been a blur since you left, but
still here are memories, all of you.

Everything you did, from beginning, until the
end, I applaud and thank you.
Never did I feel luckier to have an amazing
being like you as a mother hen.
Don't ever stop being you because even as an
angel, in the end, you are still you.

Thank you

Thank you for devotion and encouragement
throughout my life.
Haven't had anyone as unique and memorable as
yourself within my living years.
An angel called your name and elsewhere you
had to go.
Noble kings and queens had no patch on you.
Kindness and decorum, you had in droves.

You were my one, my absolute everything.
Our hearts still sing loud at the thought and
memories of you.
Understand us, we will never forget you. Thank
you.